Country File
Nigeria

Ian Graham

FRANKLIN WATTS
LONDON•SYDNEY

First published in 2004 by
Franklin Watts
96 Leonard Street, London
EC2A 4XD

Franklin Watts Australia
45–51 Huntley Street,
Alexandria, NSW 2015

COUNTRY FILE: NIGERIA produced for Franklin Watts by Bender Richardson White, PO Box 266, Uxbridge, UK.
Editor: Lionel Bender
Designer and Page Make-up: Ben White
Picture Researcher: Cathy Stastny
Cover Make-up: Mike Pilley, Radius
Production: Kim Richardson

Graphics and Maps: Stefan Chabluk

Consultant: Dr Terry Jennings, a former teacher and university lecturer. He is now a full-time writer of children's geography and science books.

A CIP catalogue record for this book is available from the British Library.

ISBN 0-7496-5382-5

Manufactured in China

Picture Credits

Pages 1, 3: Hutchison Library. 4: Robert Harding Picture Library. 6: Eye Ubiquitous/E. Neal. 8, 9: Hutchison Library/Liba Taylor. 11: Hutchison Library/Juliet Highet. 13 top: Hutchison Library. 13 bottom: Hutchison Library/Sarah Errington. 14 top: Hutchison Library. 14 bottom: Hutchison Library/Anna Tully. 16, 17, 18 top: Hutchison Library. 18 bottom: Corbis Images/Liba Taylor. 20, 21, 22, 23, 24: Hutchison Library. 25: Hutchison Library/John Goldblatt. 26: Hutchison Library/C. Saky. 26–27: Hutchison Library/Liba Taylor. 28–29: Hutchison Library/Anna Tully. 30: Robert Harding/Schuster/Hoffmann-Burch. 31: Hutchison Library.

Cover Photo: Corbis Images Inc./Paul Almasy

The Author

Ian Graham is a full-time writer and editor of non-fiction books. He has written more than 100 books for children.

Note to parents and teachers

Every effort has been made by the Publishers to ensure that the websites in this book are suitable for children, that they are of the highest educational value, and that they contain no inappropriate or offensive material. However, because of the nature of the Internet, it is impossible to guarantee that the contents of these sites will not be altered. We strongly advise that Internet access is supervised by a responsible adult.

Contents

Welcome to Nigeria

The Federal Republic of Nigeria, usually known simply as Nigeria, is the largest country of West Africa. It is larger than the US state of Texas and more than three times the size of the UK. Roughly square in shape, it is situated on the south coast of western Africa, just north of the equator.

Nigeria is known for its very large population, ethnic diversity, rich cultural heritage and varied landscape. The land ranges from mangrove swamps and tropical forests to grass-covered plains and desert. In the cities, wealth and poverty exist side by side, but the great majority of the population lives in poverty. It is a land of great potential. Its abundant mineral resources, scenic landscape and varied wildlife offer the possibility of future economic growth and development under the right leadership.

DATABASE

Neighbours

Nigeria shares borders with four other countries. Chad and Cameroon lie to its east, Benin to the west and Niger to the north. Some of these borders are in dispute. Nigeria's southern shores look out into the Gulf of Guinea, part of the Atlantic Ocean.

Lagos, Nigeria's largest city, is modern and bustling. The commercial district is crowded with office blocks, houses of worship, shops, people and traffic. ▼

The Land

Animals

Nigeria's mammals include:
Antelope, baboon, buffalo,
camel, cheetah, chimpanzee,
elephant, gazelle, giraffe,
golden cat, gorilla,
hippopotamus, hyena, jackal,
leopard, lion, rhinoceros,
serval, waterbuck, wild pig.

Birds:
Abyssinian roller, barn owl,
bee-eater, bittern, bush-
shrike, cuckoo, egret, guinea
fowl, heron, nightjar, oriole,
osprey, partridge, plover,
sandpiper, swallow, swift,
vulture, wood dove,
woodchat.

Reptiles and amphibians:
African rock python, Nile
crocodile, Nile monitor.

Nigeria can be divided into three main geographical regions. A dense forest zone extends up to 150 kilometres inland from the coast. Beyond that, there is a central savannah, or grassland, region. Further north still lies the edge of the sandy Sahel, the semi-arid region south of the Sahara Desert.

Most of Nigeria is a series of plains and plateaus. There are many hills, but the only mountains of any size are in the south-east, along the Cameroon border. The main river, the Niger, is the third longest in Africa. It rises in the Fouta Djallon hills in Guinea, more than 1,400 kilometres west of Nigeria. It flows through southern Mali and western Niger into Nigeria. The main tributary of the Niger, the Benue, flows into it at Lokoja. The Niger continues south and flows out into the Gulf of Guinea.

Small villages line the banks of the Niger for most of its length. ▼

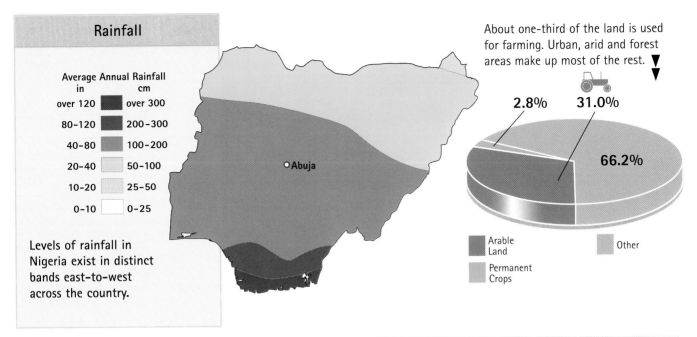

Rainfall

Average Annual Rainfall

in	cm
over 120	over 300
80–120	200–300
40–80	100–200
20–40	50–100
10–20	25–50
0–10	0–25

Levels of rainfall in Nigeria exist in distinct bands east-to-west across the country.

Abuja

About one-third of the land is used for farming. Urban, arid and forest areas make up most of the rest.

2.8% 31.0%

66.2%

Arable Land

Permanent Crops

Other

Lake Chad

The largest lake, Lake Chad, is shared by Nigeria, Cameroon, Niger and Chad. It has shrunk dramatically in recent decades. In the 1960s, it occupied an area of about 25,000 square kilometres. Now, it is barely one-twentieth of that size. The lake is very shallow (less than 7 metres), so small changes in depth have a great effect on its area. It is shrinking because of increasing demands for irrigation and decreasing rainfall.

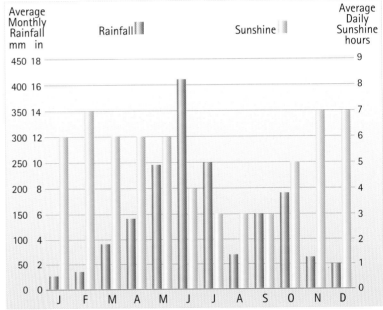

Climate

Southern Nigeria has four seasons – the long rainy season from March to July; the short dry season in August; the short rainy season from September to mid-October; and the long dry season from late October to early March. In the north, there are two seasons – the long dry season from October to May and the wet season from June to September. Rainfall varies from about 65 centimetres a year in the north-east to more than 330 centimetres at the coast.

▲ Climate details for Lagos, on the south-west coast, where rainfall is highest between May and July and daily sunshine longest from November to June.

The People

Nigeria has the largest population of any African country and it is increasing quickly. It is also one of the most diverse populations, made up from more than 300 ethnic groups.

People from practically all the native races of Africa live in Nigeria. Of these, the Hausa, Yoruba and Igbo (also called Ibo) peoples make up about 40 per cent of the population. The Hausa people live mainly in the north-west, the Yoruba in the south-west and the Igbo in the south. The Hausa are sometimes called Hausa-Fulani, because they include some of the Fulani people who are scattered all over west Africa. They entered the Hausa lands in the 19th century and many of them adopted the Hausa language and culture.

DATABASE

Ancient history

The full story of early human settlements in Nigeria has yet to be determined, because little archaeological work has been done. The oldest human remains found so far have been dated to about 9,000 BCE. The earliest known civilization or culture to develop in Nigeria is the Nok people who lived mainly on the central Jos plateau from about 500 BCE to 200 CE.

Igbo girls at a street market in Abuja, the capital of Nigeria. ▼

Many of the Hausa people in the north practise the Muslim religion and wear traditional Arab clothing. ►►

Languages
More than 400 native languages are spoken in Nigeria. The most widespread are Hausa, Yoruba and Igbo. Hausa is spoken in northern Nigeria and throughout much of western Africa. Yoruba is spoken by about 20 million people in Nigeria and the neighbouring countries of Benin and Togo to the west. Igbo is spoken by about 20 million people in southern Nigeria

Most Nigerians speak more than one language. The official language, English, is widely spoken as a second language, especially by educated people. Trade between different ethnic groups who speak different languages is carried on in Hausa in the north and pidgin in the south. Pidgin is a mixture of words from English and native Nigerian languages.

There are more men than women in Nigeria. ►►

50.4%

49.6%

Female Population
59,496,000

Male Population
60,550,000

9

Urban and Rural Life

The Forest People

Small groups of people live in the forests of southern Nigeria, deliberately hiding away from the rest of the population. They are people who suffer from leprosy. Leprosy is a disease that can result in the loss of fingers and toes, and disfigurement of the face. Lepers are often shunned by other people, so many of them choose to live together, away from the rest of the population.

Nigeria's cities are busy and modern. The streets are full of cars. Thousands of people fill the shops and offices. Outside the cities, life for ordinary Nigerians is very different. Rural areas often lack basic amenities and services such as clean water and electric power.

Nigeria's most modern city is its capital, Abuja. Its construction began in the 1980s. Its location in the middle of the country was chosen so that no ethnic group, or its homeland, were seen to be favoured at the expense of any other. Abuja became the official capital in 1991.

In the towns and cities, shops and businesses open from 8.00 a.m. to 5.00 or 6.00 p.m usually Monday to Saturday. Local markets stay open longer hours, until about 7.00 p.m. Some of them have a late-opening night, when they remain open until as late as midnight.

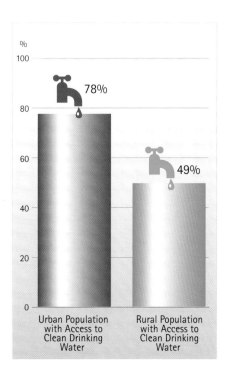

◄◄ Less than half of Nigeria's rural population has access to clean drinking water.

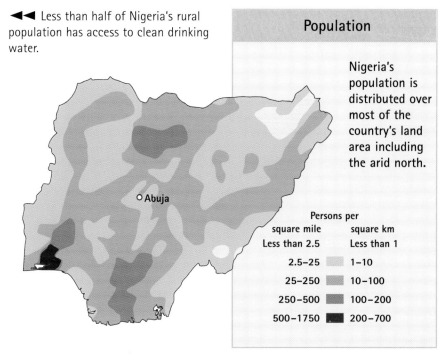

Population

Nigeria's population is distributed over most of the country's land area including the arid north.

Persons per	
square mile	square km
Less than 2.5	Less than 1
2.5–25	1–10
25–250	10–100
250–500	100–200
500–1750	200–700

Rural life

Outside the major cities, most Nigerians struggle to survive on less than 70 pence a day. There are few roads, little clean running water, no electricity and no telephones. Bicycles are essential for transport. People ride them but also wheel them along piled high with firewood or sacks of produce for sale at the local market. Bicycles are also used as taxis. Up to four people are sometimes carried on one bicycle!

Law and order

In the towns and cities, law and order is maintained by the police and courts, enforcing laws enacted by parliament. In rural areas, the same laws apply, but problems, disputes and some crimes are often dealt with by local chiefs, village elders and religious leaders.

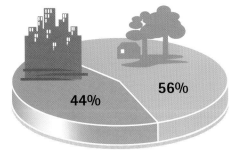

44%   56%

■ Percentage of Population Living in Urban Areas

■ Percentage of Population Living in Rural Areas

▲ Less than half of Nigeria's people live in towns and cities.

In urban and rural areas, many people buy food, clothes and household items, such as pots and pans, from stalls in street markets like this one in Lagos. ▼

🌐 **Web Search** ▶▶

▶ http://www.greatest cities.com/Africa/ Nigeria/Abuja_city_ state_capital.html
Information about Nigeria's capital city, Abuja.

▶ http://news.bbc.co.uk/ 1/hi/world/africa/ 3043627.stm
An article about Nigeria's forest-dwelling leprosy sufferers, from BBC News.

▶ http://www.e-nigeria. info/biz.htm
General information on Nigeria including its bank, shop and business opening hours.

Farming and Fishing

Nigeria's varied climate and plentiful rain in the south allow a wide variety of crops to be grown. Nearly three-quarters of the population work in agriculture. Even so, farm production has not kept pace with the growth of the population. As a result, Nigeria, which was once self-sufficient in food, must now import food.

Some crops are grown for food, while others are cash crops, grown to be sold to other countries. The main food crops are cassava, maize, rice, yams and various vegetables and beans. The main cash crops are cocoa, cotton, groundnuts, oil palm and rubber.

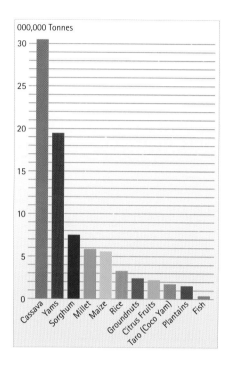

◄◄ By weight of produce, cassava and yams are the most important crops. The output of the fishing industry is tiny by comparison to farming.

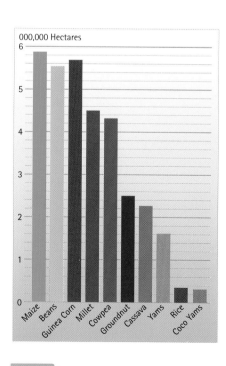

◄◄ In terms of area of farmland given over to particular crops, maize, beans and corn are the most important.

Farming regions

Crops are grown mainly on fertile river plains. Goats are herded on the hills. In the north, spreading desert is destroying farmland. Elsewhere, uncontrolled forest clearance and over-grazing has also led to soil erosion.

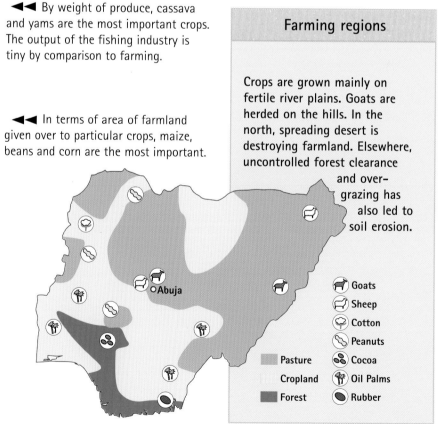

🐐 Goats
🐑 Sheep
🌿 Cotton
🥜 Peanuts
🍫 Cocoa
🌴 Oil Palms
⚫ Rubber

Pasture
Cropland
Forest

◄◄ Workers load sacks of groundnuts (peanuts) on to a lorry to be taken to market for export.

Fishing

Most of Nigeria's fishing catch is produced from its rivers, lakes and coastal waters by people using small boats, little equipment and traditional methods. Commercial fishing and fish farming account for about one-tenth of the total catch of fish, shrimps and eels.

Arable farming

Most farms are small but with government help are getting larger and more efficient. Different crops are grown in each part of the country to suit the local climate. Groundnuts, cotton, sugar cane, rice, wheat and tobacco are grown in the north. Cocoa, rubber, palm oil and kola nuts are grown in the south, where the Niger River delta provides a large expanse of fertile land. Beniseed, ginger and yams are grown across the central belt. Nigeria is also one of the world's biggest producers of tropical timbers. About 124 million tonnes of timber are produced every year.

Many villagers support their families by fishing in local rivers. ▼

Livestock farming

Most of the country's cattle, sheep and goats are raised in the central belt, which offers the best conditions for them. To the north, there is not enough water for the animals. In the warmer south, insect pests such as the tsetse fly thrive. Tsetse flies are blood-sucking insects that infect people and animals with a disease, called sleeping sickness in humans and nagana in animals.

Web Search ►►

► http://www.nigeria businessinfo.com/agric-data.htm
Data on agriculture in Nigeria.

Resources and Industry

Nigeria's industries are poorly developed. The country's troubled past, corruption and political instability have discouraged many foreign companies from working and investing there. Its economy relies heavily on exports of oil and natural gas.

Oil and gas are Nigeria's most valuable minerals. They bring in about 90 per cent of the country's export earnings. They are produced mainly in the Niger Delta basin and offshore in the Gulf of Guinea. Nigeria is Africa's largest oil producer, just ahead of Libya, and the world's tenth-largest oil producer.

Despite having such valuable resources, corruption and mismanagement have left Nigeria as one of the world's 20 poorest countries. It exports about 2 million barrels of oil every day, but its oil refineries have been left to decay. As a result, Nigeria has to import almost three-quarters of the fuel it needs even though it has rich supplies of oil.

▲ An oil rig in swampland near Port Harcourt on the coast. Nigeria is a member of OPEC, the international Organization of Petroleum Exporting Countries.

In a plastics factory, a worker puts covers on cans of aerosol spray. Many jobs are done by low-paid workers rather than by machines. ►►

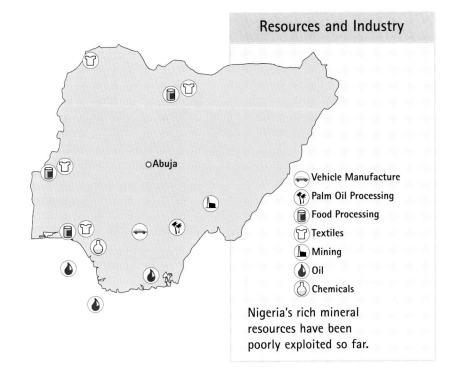

Power Problems

Industry needs electricity to power its machines and lighting. Without electricity, the country's many textile and footwear producers, vehicle assembly companies and other manufacturers cannot produce anything. The electrical supply in Nigeria has been so unreliable in recent years that many companies have installed their own private power generating equipment. However, the engines that drive the generators need fuel. Fuel shortages mean that even the privately owned generators cannot work.

Resources and Industry

Vehicle Manufacture
Palm Oil Processing
Food Processing
Textiles
Mining
Oil
Chemicals

Nigeria's rich mineral resources have been poorly exploited so far.

The majority of Nigerians work in agriculture. 'Services' include finance, banking and insurance. ▶▶

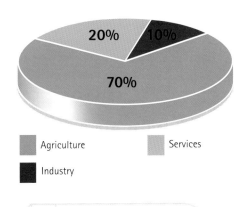

20%   10%

70%

Agriculture   Services

Industry

Limestone

In addition to oil and natural gas, there are extensive deposits of limestone throughout the country. They supply Nigeria's many cement factories. Tin, iron ore, lead and zinc are mined, too, and Nigeria is the only west African country to produce coal. It was discovered in 1909 and commercial mining began in 1916 near Enugu. Known coal reserves stand at about 2 billion tonnes.

Industrial training

Opportunities for training in industry are limited within Nigeria itself, so young Nigerians have traditionally gone abroad for training in a wide variety of industries. Every year, about 2,000 of them return home to use their skills and training in Nigeria's developing industries.

Web Search ▶▶

► http://minerals.usgs.gov/minerals/pubs/country/2001/nimyb01.pdf

Information about Nigeria's minerals industry from the US Geological Survey.

Transport

Nigeria has a very poor transport system. There was very little investment in transport during the 15 years when the country was under military rule. Since then, the civilian government has pledged to improve transport.

Despite the country's vast oil reserves, petrol has often been in short supply, especially during the years of military rule in the 1980s and 1990s. Petrol shortages are less common today, but they still happen. When they do, they bring road transport to a standstill as drivers wait for hours in long queues at fuel stations. Even during shortages, petrol is available on the black market, but most Nigerians cannot afford the highly inflated prices.

Air and Sea

Most of Nigeria's long-haul passenger and cargo traffic enter and leave the country through its international airports at Lagos, Kano and Abuja, and its main seaports at Lagos, Warri, Port Harcourt, Onne and Calabar. Passenger ferries also carry people between ports on the Gulf of Guinea.

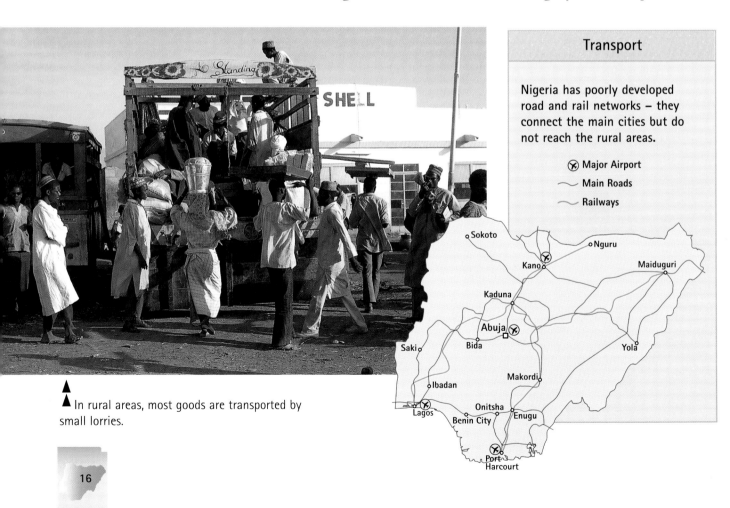

▲ In rural areas, most goods are transported by small lorries.

Transport

Nigeria has poorly developed road and rail networks – they connect the main cities but do not reach the rural areas.

- ⊗ Major Airport
- ╲ Main Roads
- ╲ Railways

Sokoto · Nguru · Kano · Maiduguri · Kaduna · Abuja · Saki · Bida · Yola · Ibadan · Makordi · Lagos · Onitsha · Enugu · Benin City · Port Harcourt

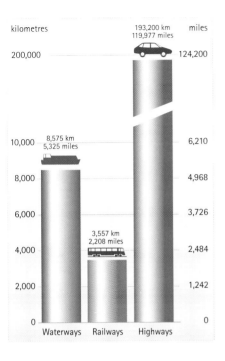

kilometres		193,200 km 119,977 miles	miles

Waterways   Railways   Highways

▲
Only about 15,000 km of Nigeria's roads are paved intercity all-weather roads. River transport is very important.

Buses

The most common way to get around in big cities such as Lagos is by one of the 1,000 or more distinctive yellow buses, called *molues* and *danfos*. The larger molues have seating for 44 passengers, but dozens more often crowd onto them and stand tightly packed together. The smaller danfos can seat 12 people, but they are often overcrowded, too. Bus fares are cheap, but the seating is uncomfortable and many of the buses are in poor condition.

Railways

Nigeria's railways were built by Britain in the nineteenth century. Lines run south from Nguru, Maiduguri and Kaura-Namoda in the north to Lagos and Port Harcourt on the south coast. Successive governments have failed to invest in the railway network, so it is in a very poor state. In 2002, the government announced a 25-year plan to modernize the railways at a cost of £38 billion.

◀◀ Flyovers in Lagos are often crowded with tanker lorries, trucks, cars and buses. Volumes of traffic are heaviest around ports and oil refineries along the coast.

Web Search ▶▶

▶ http://www.nigerian embassy.ru/Nigeria/ economy.htm

A profile of Nigeria from one of its embassies, with details of its ports, airports, road network and railways (and other economy topics).

17

Education

Mobile Classrooms

Nomadic people travel with their herds, looking for fresh pastures. It has been difficult to provide them with education because of their constant movement around the country. The government has tried to improve the education service to nomads by building schools in the places they visit most often and supplying mobile classrooms that can travel with them. A mobile classroom and its furniture can be dismantled within 30 minutes and carried by pack animals, trucks or motor caravans.

Children in Nigeria are educated in one of three ways. There is a European-style national education system, common in many cities. There are Islamic schools, especially in the northern states. In rural areas, where there are fewer schools, children may be educated informally in the traditional way.

Children in Nigerian villages have been taught about their history, customs and practical skills by parents and village elders for generations. Islamic communities added formal classes in religious studies and their holy book, the *Koran*. Europeans introduced a formal educational system in the nineteenth century. All of these systems and methods, formal and informal, continue in Nigeria today.

Stages of education

In the towns and cities, pre-primary or nursery education is available privately to some children aged 3 to 5 years. Primary school begins at the age of 6. There are private schools and state schools. Primary school ends at the age of 11. Secondary school education lasts for 6 years. There are two stages of 3 years each – Junior Secondary School and Senior Secondary School.

Children can leave school after Junior Secondary stage and, if they wish, go on to take an apprenticeship or some other form of practical training. The most able students who complete Senior Secondary School can go on to study at a university, polytechnic or college of technology.

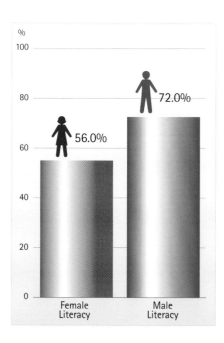

%

100	
80	72.0%
60	56.0%
40	
20	
0	
Female Literacy	Male Literacy

◄◄ Literacy levels are considerably lower among women.

Some Secondary Schools have very modern buildings and facilities, as here in the computer room of a school in Abuja, but many schools are old and poorly maintained. ►►

44.1%

55.9%

Male/Female Primary School Pupils
Total 16,191,000

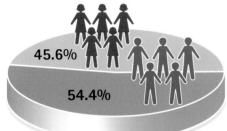

45.6%

54.4%

Male/Female Secondary School Pupils
Total 4,451,000

▲ Number of pupils – primary and secondary. The percentage of boys being educated is higher at all levels of education.

In most European-style primary schools, children work at desks. ▶▶

🌐 **Web Search** ▶▶

▶ http://unstats.un.org/ unsd/demographic/ social/illiteracy.htm
Information about literacy levels in various countries, including Nigeria, from the United Nations.

▶ http://www.nigerian embassy.ru/Nigeria/ education.htm
Information about education in Nigeria from one of its embassies.

Sport and Leisure

Nigerians are sports-loving people. The country's athletes have competed at the highest level in international sports and won medals and championships against the best in the world.

Football is the most popular sport in Nigeria. Primary and Secondary Schools, colleges and even some private companies have football teams. Clubs compete each year for several trophies. The most important of them is the Nigeria Challenge Cup. Nigerian teams also compete against teams from all over Africa for the Mandela Cup. The national team has won the African Nations Cup and Nigeria's women's football team has won the Africa Champions Cup three times.

Boxing and athletics

After football, boxing is the next most popular sport. Nigeria has produced three world champions – Hogan 'Kid' Bassey (featherweight) in the 1950s, Dick Tiger (middleweight) in the 1960s and Bash Ali (cruiserweight) in the 1980s. Ayo, a type of wrestling, is a popular traditional sport in villages.

Nigeria is also well known for table tennis, lawn tennis, basketball, athletics and hockey. Its athletes have won Olympic medals in several track and field events. Nigeria won its first Olympic gold medals at the 1996 Olympic Games in Atlanta, USA.

Eyo Festival

The main festival in Lagos is the Eyo festival. The city centre is closed as a procession passes through and pays homage to the Oba (Yoruba king) of Lagos. A new Oba was selected by six king-makers in March 2003 after the reigning Oba died at the age of 92.

Horseracing is growing again in popularity, especially in north Nigeria, after many years of neglect. ▼

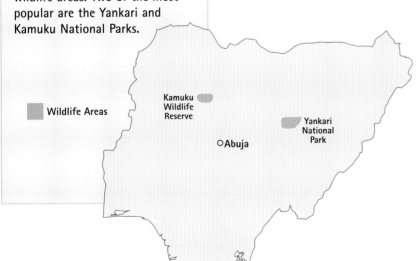

▲ Youngsters will play football – often barefoot – on any open space, as in this marketplace in central Lagos.

National Parks

Some Nigerians, like tourists, enjoy exploring the country's wildlife areas. Two of the most popular are the Yankari and Kamuku National Parks.

Wildlife Areas

Kamuku Wildlife Reserve

Yankari National Park

○Abuja

Festivals

One of Nigeria's most colourful festivals is the Argungu fishing festival. It is held every year in Argungu, about 100 kilometres from Sokoto, to mark the beginning of the freshwater fishing season. Men in boats beat drums and rattle gourds filled with seeds to drive fish into shallow water. There, more than 1,000 men and boys are waiting in the water with nets.

Web Search ▶▶

▶ http://www.africa online.com/site/ng/ sports.jsp
Information about Nigerian sports provided by a pan-Africa site.

Daily Life and Religion

Religion plays an important part in daily life in much of Nigeria. Many of the rituals, customs and practices observed in everyday activities are rooted in religious beliefs.

The people are mostly Muslim in the north of the country and Christian in the south. Eight of Nigeria's northern states have introduced Islamic law. The Islamic legal code, or Sharia, imposes harsh punishments, including stoning, flogging and amputating hands. Boys and girls must be educated separately. Men and women are forbidden from travelling together on public transport and from drinking alcohol. The introduction of Sharia led to violence between Muslim and Christian communities.

Only about one in ten Nigerians follows traditional African religions. These often involve ancestor worship or animism, a belief in the existence of spirits in daily life.

Muslim worshippers gather for daily prayers at a mosque in Kano. ▼

Food

Nigerian families usually eat together at home. More than enough food is made in case visitors call in. Cooked meals can also be bought at roadside stalls called *buka*.

Nigerian dishes are mostly based on grains, such as maize and millet. Hot, peppery stews are popular in the southern part of the country. Traditional Hausa food includes *tuo shinkafa*, made from mashed rice grain, and *tuo masara*, made from mashed corn grain, served with soup. Yoruba food includes *Iyan*, made from pounded yam, and *amala*, made from cassava or yam flour, served with soup.

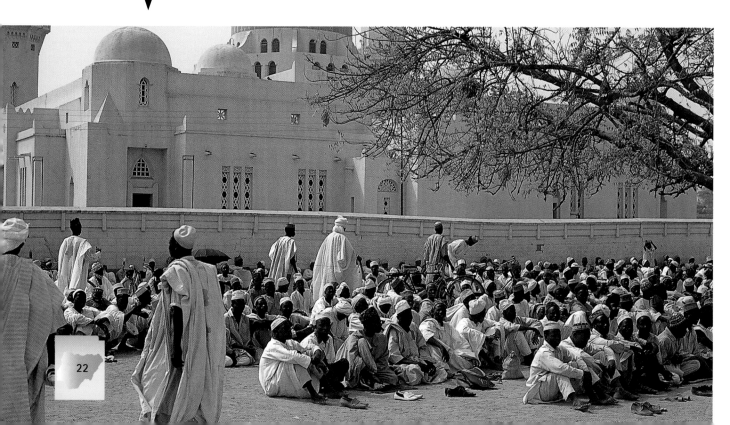

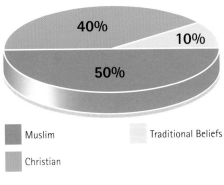

Muslim   Traditional Beliefs

Christian

▲▲ Muslims make up the largest religious group.

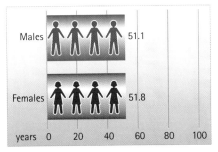

▲▲ Fulani herdsmen in the dry Sahel region wear a loose-fitting buba and a fila to help keep them cool in the heat of day. They carry wrap-round blankets for warmth at night.

▲▲ Life expectancy in Nigeria is very low due to poor healthcare and medical services.

Dress

Suits, dresses and casual western-style clothes are common, but traditional African dress and Arab-style clothing are worn, too. The brightly coloured African garments are known by different names in different parts of the country. Men wear a loose, comfortable shirt that reaches down to the knees, known as a *buba* in the Yoruba language, over trousers called *sokoto*. A cap called a *fila* may be worn. On important occasions, men may also wear a long, wide-sleeved robe called an *agbada*. Women wear a long wrap-around skirt called an *iro*, a short-sleeved top called a *buba*, similar to the men's shirt of the same name, and a head-scarf called a *gele*. Many children dress in similar clothing and styles.

Web Search ►►

► http://unstats.un.org/ unsd/demographic/ social/health.htm
Life expectancy information from the United Nations for a variety of countries including Nigeria

► http://www.mapzones. com/world/africa/nigeria/ cultureindex.php
Information from a travel and tourist organization.

Arts and Media

Art, music and dance are important in Nigerian life. Nigeria's artists, performers and media enjoy greater freedom today than they did under a succession of repressive military regimes.

Nigerian art can be traced back more than 2,000 years. Nigerian artists and craft workers are expert in wood carving, leatherwork, weaving and working in copper and bronze. Highly decorated ceremonial masks and costumes are a speciality, too.

The media

Some newspapers are run by the state, but many others are privately owned. They are free to criticise the government if they wish to. Most Nigerians receive their news by radio. There are many national, regional and local radio stations. The state-owned Federal Radio Corporation of Nigeria runs a network of radio stations. In addition, Nigerians can tune in to international broadcasts. There are national and regional television stations to choose from, too. The Nigerian Television Authority is the state-owned national television service.

In such a big country, radio is the best way to keep up to date with news. Nigerians own more than 23 million radio sets – almost one per family. ▼

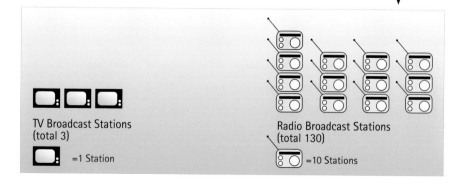

TV Broadcast Stations
(total 3)

☐ =1 Station

Radio Broadcast Stations
(total 130)

[radio] =10 Stations

▲
▲ Traditional arts and crafts, such as basketry using coloured beads, and woodcarving, are popular pastimes but also ways of earning a living.

Writers

Nigerian writers have achieved international success. For example, Ben Okri's books about Nigerian society and politics have won such awards as the British Booker Prize in 1991. The playwright, novelist and poet, Wole Soyinka, was imprisoned in the 1960s for his writing. In 1986, he became the first black African to win the Nobel Prize for literature.

Nigerian Ken Saro-Wiwa became as famous for his human rights activities as for his writing. He campaigned against the government and oil companies who, he said, had damaged his Ogoni homeland in the Niger Delta. He was executed along with eight supporters in 1995. This led to the condemnation of Nigeria by the international community, the imposition of trade sanctions and suspension from the Commonwealth.

Overseas Visitors

Nigeria's magnificent scenery, varied wildlife, national parks, game reserves and over 700 km of sandy beaches should make it a major attraction for tourists. However, its troubled past, political instability and under-developed transport networks have discouraged tourists from visiting in large numbers.

◄◄ In his paintings, present-day Nigerian artist, Aderisi Fabhnmi, shows the influence of both traditional African and contemporary western styles.

Web Search ►►

► http://e-nigeria.info/social.htm
A survey of the arts in Nigeria.

► http://www.bbc.co.uk/arts/books/author/okri
Information about the Nigerian writer Ben Okri from the BBC.

► http://www.tvradioworld.com/region3/nig/
A survey of Nigeria's tv and radio broadcasting stations.

Government

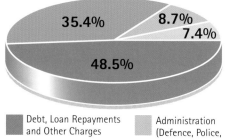

35.4%   8.7%
7.4%
48.5%

- Debt, Loan Repayments and Other Charges
- Economic Services (Transport, Science, Communication, Power, etc)
- Administration (Defence, Police, General Government Expenses, etc)
- Social and Communication Services (Education, Housing, Tourism, etc)

▲ How the Nigerian government spends money each year. Unfortunately, the largest proportion goes towards paying off loans and debts.

▲ City planners study scale models and maps for a new development in Abuja. The government funds many building programmes across the nation.

Nigeria was governed by Britain until it became an independent country in 1960. Six years later, a coup brought a military leadership to power. Several more coups and a war later, a new government was elected in 1979. Military forces seized power again in 1983. Democracy returned with new parliamentary and presidential elections as recently as 1999.

Nigeria's parliament is called the National Assembly. It has an upper house, called the Senate, with 109 seats, and a lower house, called the House of Representatives, with 360 seats. Senators and Representatives are elected by the people for a four-year term of office.

The president

The president is the head of state, head of government, and commander-in-chief of the armed forces. He or she is elected for four years and may not serve more than two four-year terms. The president governs at the head of the Federal Executive Council of ministers, who are appointed by the president. A member of the National Assembly must resign from it before becoming a minister.

The meeting place in Abuja of ECOWAS, the Economic Community of West African States, of which Nigeria is a member. ►►

Local government

Each state has its own governor, elected for four years. The governor is the chief executive of the state's House of Assembly, which is made up of local government representatives and is responsible for making regional laws. At an even more local level, there are 774 local government areas, each administered by a council. The councils are responsible for local services including collecting local taxes and building roads. They also share responsibility with the state governments for providing primary education and health services.

Government

Nigeria is made up of 36 states and 1 territory. The capital city, Abuja, is located in the Federal Capital Territory in the centre of the country.

 Web Search ►►

► http://www.economist.com
Website of The Economist *magazine, with a 'Country Briefing' on Nigeria.*

► http://www.onlinenigeria.com/links/adv.asp?blurb=138
Details of Nigeria's government.

► http://news.bbc.co.uk/1/hi/world/africa/country_profiles/1067695.stm
A timeline of events in Nigeria, from BBC News.

Place in the World

11th –14th centuries Hausa city-states develop in northern Nigeria. Yoruba cities including Ife, Oyo and Benin, become important trading centres.

14th century Islam is introduced from the Mali empire in north-west Africa.

15th century Trade with Portugal begins.

17th-18th centuries The slave trade is at its peak.

1820s The British Royal Navy intercepts slave ships, frees the slaves and takes them to Sierra Leone.

1851 British military forces shell Lagos and expel the Oba (king).

1861 Britain takes control of Lagos.

1886 Lagos becomes a British colony.

1903 The British overcome Fulani states in northern Nigeria and capture the cities of Kano and Sokoto.

1914 Britain's protectorates in Nigeria are combined to form the Colony and Protectorate of Nigeria. The Nigerian Legislative Council is formed.
World War I begins. Nigerian forces invade German-held Kamerun (Cameroon).

1923 Herbert Macaulay establishes the first Nigerian political party, the Nigerian National Democratic Party.

1960 Nigeria gains its independence from Britain.

1961 The northern part of the Trust Territory of the Cameroons joins Nigeria's Northern Region. The Southern Cameroons joins Cameroun to form the Federal Republic of Cameroon.

Nigeria's relations with the rest of the world were strained during the years of military rule, but they have improved since democracy was restored in 1999.

The demands of Nigeria's enormous population present the government with a daunting challenge. The need to modernize the country's road and rail networks and develop new industries after decades of neglect cannot be done by Nigeria alone. Massive international investment and funding and the involvement of foreign companies and governments are needed.

To attract private investors and increased aid from other countries, Nigeria will have to deal more effectively with the mismanagement, corruption, civil disturbances and crime that have discouraged many of them in the past.

President Obasanjo (in blue) greets government representatives at a ceremony celebrating the introduction of Nigeria's modern constitution. ▼

International links

Nigeria belongs to a large number of international organizations, including the African, Caribbean and Pacific Group of States (ACP), the International Olympic Committee (IOC), the United Nations (UN), UNESCO (the United Nations Educational, Scientific and Cultural Organization), the World Trade Organization and the World Health Organization (WHO).

International disputes

In 2002, one of these organizations, the International Court of Justice, considered Nigeria's dispute with Cameroon over the oil-rich Bakassi Peninsula in the Gulf of Guinea. Its decision was that Nigeria should hand over the peninsula to Cameroon. The Nigerian government and the people who live on the peninsula rejected the ruling and refused to hand over the land. This dispute continues.

Nigeria's imports and exports. ▼▼

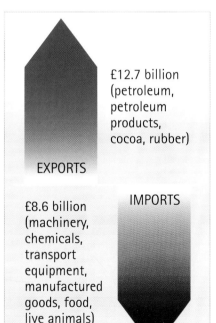

EXPORTS
£12.7 billion (petroleum, petroleum products, cocoa, rubber)

IMPORTS
£8.6 billion (machinery, chemicals, transport equipment, manufactured goods, food, live animals)

Area:
923,768 sq km

Population size:
129,934,950

Capital city:
Abuja
(Population 339,100)

Other major cities:
Lagos (pop. 2,500,000)
Ibadan (pop. 1,365,000)
Kano (pop. 657,300)
Kaduna (pop. 333,600)

Longest rivers:
Niger (4,200 km, of which roughly
one-third lies within Nigeria)

Highest mountain:
Chappal Waddi (2,419 m)

Currency:
1 naira (N) = 100 kobo
£1 = 225N

Languages:
English (official), Yoruba, Ibo,
Hausa and about 400 other
African languages

Flag:
Three equal vertical bands of
green, white and green

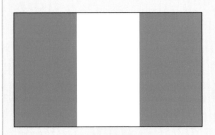

Major resources:
Natural gas, petroleum, tin, iron
ore, coal, limestone, lead, zinc,
arable land, timber

Major exports:
Petroleum (crude oil), petroleum
products, cocoa, rubber, timber,
animal hides

Some holidays and major events:
January 1: New Year's Day
May 1: Worker's Day

May 27: Children's Day
October 1: Independence Day
December 25: Christmas Day
There are Muslim holidays, too,
but as these are based on the
lunar calendar, their date on the
solar calendar changes each year

Religions:
Islam, Christianity, traditional
African beliefs

Glossary

AGRICULTURE
Farming the land, including ploughing, planting, raising crops and raising animals.

BLACK MARKET
The illegal, uncontrolled and corrupt trade in goods, usually to avoid paying taxes or for things in short supply.

CLIMATE
The long-term weather in an area.

CONTINENT
One of the Earth's largest land masses – Europe, Asia, Australia, North and South America, Africa and Antarctica.

COUP
Short for the French *coup d'etat*, a violent or illegal replacement of a country's government.

CULTURE
The beliefs, ideas, knowledge and customs of a group of people, or the group of people themselves.

DESERTIFICATION
The spreading of deserts into neighbouring areas due to climate change and erosion of the soil by poor farming and poor water management.

ECONOMY
A country's finances.

EXPORTS
Products, resources or goods sold to other countries.

GOVERNMENT
A group of people who manage a country, deciding on laws, raising taxes and organizing health, education, transport and other national systems and services.

GROSS DOMESTIC PRODUCT
The value of all goods and services produced by a nation in a year.

IMPORTS
Products, resources or goods brought into the country.

LITERACY
The ability to read and write.

LITERACY RATE
The percentage of the population who can read and write.

MANUFACTURING
Making large numbers of the same things by hand or, more commonly, by machine.

POPULATION
All the people who live in a city, country, region or other area.

POPULATION DENSITY
The average number of people living in each square kilometre of a city, country, region or other area.

RESOURCES
Materials that can be used to make goods or electricity, or to generate income for a country or region.

RURAL
Having the qualities of the countryside, with a low population density.

URBAN
Having the qualities of a city, with a high population density.

A villager prepares to dye clothes in a pit dug in the ground and filled with indigo extracted from plants. This is a traditional way of dyeing clothes, practised for many centuries. ▼
▼

Index